# INSPIRATION: TAKE LIFE ONE STEP AT A TIME

Sylvia Carlton

BK Royston Publishing
P. O. Box 4321
Jeffersonville, IN 47131
502-802-5385
http://www.bkroystonpublishing.com
bkroystonpublishing@gmail.com

© Copyright – 2020

All Rights Reserved. No part of this book may be reproduced, stored in a retrieval system, or transmitted by any means without the written permission of the author.

Cover Design: Gad Elite Cover Designs

ISBN: 978-1-946111-75-3

Printed in the United States of America

# Dedication

This book is dedicated to my parents, who were my greatest inspiration.

# Table of Contents

| | |
|---|---|
| Dedication | iii |
| The Birth of This Book | vii |
| Part One: Bits and Pieces | 1 |
| Part Two: Thoughts To Consider | 19 |
| Part Three: Month By Month Encouragement | 27 |
| Part Four: # LovingJoe #IWillSurvive | 41 |
| Final Thoughts | 51 |
| Excerpt from the Novel "Colors" | 55 |

## THE BIRTH OF THIS BOOK

It has been quite a long journey to reach this point. Life for all of us has its ups and downs, crooks and turns, missteps and detours. It is all in the way that we navigate that determines the outcome.

We all know that there is light at the end of the tunnel. Although sometimes tunnels may seem to go on for miles -- even country miles -- indeed there is an entrance and, more importantly, an exit. A tunnel is a passageway through or under something; usually an obstruction. While passing through, it can be dark for a long while, but then as the darkness closes behind you, the light breaks through, signaling the end of the tunnel. It is impossible for the darkness to extend beyond the mouth of the tunnel; it will not follow you out of the tunnel, for darkness and light cannot co-exist. During the entire year of 2015, I posted on my Facebook page at the beginning of each month a short blurb, if you will, coining a phrase from Oprah, entitled "What I Know For Sure." Since this is a published work, I cannot use that quote, but I will share all 12 of those posts within this writing in the section entitled, "Month By Month Encouragement." I will also share other thoughts, including a short section dedicated to my nephew Joe-Joe, and as an extra special bonus, an excerpt from my upcoming first novel entitled "Colors" which was the book that I initially started writing some time ago. But not to worry – it will follow very shortly. You have my word on that.

Yes, it has been a long road, but it could have been shortened substantially, and that was totally up to me. I believe we all possess certain gifts. I always had a gift and a love for writing. As a child, I can remember having a wildly vivid imagination. I thought 'outside the box' even before that phrase became popular. By the time I reached middle school, I was writing college papers for friends and family. Had I thought to charge a fee, I would have had quite a hefty bank account by now. I guess I didn't have the right agent.

Over the years, life got busy and I put my writing on the back burner. BIG MISTAKE. But then isn't hindsight always 20/20?

Just prior to starting this book, I was in a bad financial state. This was particularly difficult for me since I had always been stable enough to take care of myself and even help others. I was having a pity party, complete with balloons, streamers, ice cream and cake. It was then that my niece, Karen, came to me and said okay, so you have no job, no money, no computer, no vehicle. Big deal. You are sitting here day in and day out doing absolutely nothing. Why don't you pick up a pen and paper and start writing? I looked at her for a long moment, and as much as I hated to, I had to admit that she was right. So, I popped the balloons and took down the streamers. I ate the ice cream and cake (couldn't let that go to waste) and started writing the old-fashioned way – with pen and paper on a big old writing pad.

What a wake-up call this was! I realized that I was holding myself back. Notice I did not say I was being held back, because no one can stop you but YOU. This revelation alone propelled me clear into space. I went into cartoon super speed mode. I started writing for hours on end, filling up several pages a day. No matter that I did not own a computer or couldn't always gain access to one. I made it to the local library when I could and used the computer lab. When that was not possible, I sat at the table and wrote. I sat in church and wrote (not during the sermon, mind you), I sat in the bathroom and wrote, and yes, I wrote at 3:00 a.m. in the morning. Every writer knows that when ideas come in the wee hours, you must put them on paper, otherwise by daybreak they will be clear across town.

I wrote several short stories (which will also be part of a future publication) and I wrote chapters for my novel "Colors." I switched back and forth between writings, because the characters in my head were all demanding to be heard, so I had to accommodate them all as best I could. Ultimately, since "Inspiration" was the shortest writing, it made it to the delivery room first.

During the time of this writing, I also suffered a brief setback -- a horrific incident that occurred in January of 2016 that resulted in the loss of my nephew. It was then that a very dear friend, Everlene Hampton, talked me down off the cliff. She purchased a journal for me and said "write -- no matter what." That was just the push that I needed to keep going. (I will expand upon this further in Part Four).

Thanks are in order, because as with any birthing process, there is always a team involved. Thanks first of all to my parents, Sim and Hallie Carlton, for bringing me into this world. Although they are no longer with us, their memory and everything they taught me continues to encourage and inspire me. Big thanks to my oldest sister, Colie, for helping to raise me and for always being there, and to my sister Katie for being my good email buddy. I give honor to the memory of my sister Betty, who always set a wonderful example for me. Thanks to my two brothers, Simmie and Curtis for being an integral part of my life. To my sister, Doris, I say thanks for proofreading all my material even though that had to be a huge spoiler alert. I would be remiss not to mention my late Aunt Gussie, who also had a love for words (the greatest Scrabble player ever) and my late Aunt Ella who had a style all of her own. I honestly believe that I inherited some of my writing skills from these two. They were very articulate. To the memory of my Uncle J.B., thank you for stepping in after daddy was gone. Thanks to my Aunt Ann, such a classy lady and an amazing role model, and my Uncle Tubbie for always being someone I can talk to.

So, there you have it, dear readers. The birth of this book. It is aptly titled "Inspiration" because my hope is that it will encourage and inspire. It is my thoughts, my truth, and I am honored to share it with you. I hope that you enjoy reading it as much as I enjoyed writing it. Happy reading, and I will check back in with you after the Final Thoughts.

## PART ONE

## BITS AND PIECES

*****************************

### People Make The World Go Round

People-watching can be quite fascinating. I have done that quite a bit, and found myself thinking, 'Where are they coming from? Where are they headed? What is their relationship to each other?' Sometimes seeing couples together makes me laugh out loud, because they seem to be the most unlikely match in the world. Yet, our diversity and differences are what make it such a wonderful world. I remember an assignment from one college course – Ethical Relativism – where we had to actually approach a stranger and ask them just a few questions about their life and their culture. Nothing too personal; just generally who they were and where they came from. (Mind you, this was over 30 years ago, so you could pretty much safely approach someone on the street.) At any rate, the point of the assignment was to compare our first impression of them with their actual truth. I would always approach the person with a smile. I have traveled extensively, and although there may be language barriers, a smile is the same in any language. It is the quickest and most inexpensive way to brighten someone's day. It almost always brings a smile, so you get an immediate return on your investment. Needless to say, I was almost always incorrect in what I sized up about a person from just looking at them compared to what their actual story was. Most people were more than willing to share and even pose for pictures. It made me appreciate that no matter what your station in life, everyone has a voice and there is always something that can be learned from others. It is absolutely true that you cannot judge a book by its cover. So learn to embrace different cultures, values, opinions, views and theories. Diversity is a wonderful thing. Think about it -- this world would be quite a boring place if everyone were alike.

## Pink Slips

Some people and situations need to be dismissed from your life. Don't allow your progress to be slowed down or your energy to be sapped. Hand them a pink slip and tell them to clean out their cubicle. I can recall a time when I cared about what people thought about me to the point where I tried to please everyone. That is not to say that you should not care; but not to the point where someone else defines who you are. Don't let someone else's problem become yours. Don't let someone else's enemy become yours. Remember, misery loves company. People can feel free to voice their opinions, but be careful to let it remain just that -- THEIR opinion. Others sometimes seem to want to take on the role of counselor, judge and jury over your personal affairs. They are quick to give unsolicited advice and want you to answer any questions that they ask. But on the other hand, they would never share with you the same facts about themselves. Learn to be diplomatic in these situations. When I am asked a question that I don't want to provide an answer to, I simply ignore the question or if the person cannot take the hint and persists, I reply with "Why do you want to know?" That works every time. Let me share one of my Facebook posts which pretty much sums up an excellent attitude to adopt:

"As of today, I am downsizing the plant. We will no longer be manufacturing Stress. Everyone in the Depression Department will be laid off. There will be no Christmas Pity Party. Most of the haters were dismissed previously, but if there are a few more still around, today will be your last day. Apologies for the short notice, but you pretty much knew this was coming. I would say that I will miss you all, but that would not be a true statement. So I will just say so long, because you really have been around much too long. Going forward, I will only be working with Happiness, Optimism and a Positive Outlook."

## A Five Pound Bag of Sugar

When life gives you lemons, make lemonade. We are all familiar with that saying. And I'm quite sure everyone reading this has had to make lemonade at some point. I've had to make lemonade, Kool-Aid, coffee and tea. Oftentimes, it was not the best tasting, but I made it nonetheless and I managed to drink it. I made it because it was the hand that I had been dealt. I made it because the alternative would have been to give up, and giving up was not an option. There were times when life gave me so many lemons that I thought surely I had more than my fair share. Undoubtedly someone else's troubles had been delivered to the wrong address and ended up on my doorstep. But even though that seemed to be the case, it was not at all. I had to remember that God won't put any more on me than I can bear and if he brings me to it, he can bring me through it. So when that truckload of lemons arrived, what I decided to do was not only just make lemonade, but buy a five pound bag of

Sylvia Carlton

**sugar and make the sweetest lemonade that I could!**

## **Peel It!**

When I was about four or five years old, I developed an awful cold. I didn't often get sick, but when I did, my mother used home remedies and almost always saved herself a trip to the doctor's office. This time, however, she couldn't break the fever at home and so off to the doctor we went. Sitting in the waiting room, the woman next to me struck up a conversation. Although I was always very much a people person even as a young child, on this particular day I was not up for conversation. After engaging with me for a few minutes, the woman pulled an orange out of her purse and asked my mother if I could have it. My mother said of course, and I accepted the orange. Now all parents teach their children to say thank you, but sometimes they forget and need to be reminded. When my mother did not hear me say thank you, she looked down at me and said "What do you say to the lady?" I looked up at the woman who was smiling down at me, held up the orange with both my hands and said "Peel it!"

Sylvia Carlton

Sometimes as children of God, we may forget to say thank you. Even though we have been taught to be thankful for every blessing great or small, every now and then we might not say it. When I open my eyes every morning, I say out loud, "Thank you Lord for waking me up." Seems simple enough, but think how many people didn't wake up. How many more, even after waking up, were not able to sit up on the side of the bed. How many did not wake up in their own bed but in a hospital bed, or in a cardboard box or a tattered blanket on the street. I'm thankful each day, thankful for traveling mercies to and from work or school, thankful for transportation, be it personal or public, thankful for a sound mind and a healthy body. So much to be thankful for. So yes, even for the smallest blessings that God hands us, don't say, "Peel it." Say, "Thank you."

## Wisdom Is A Wonderful Thing

Tyrone Davis penned a song that went something like this:

*Oh darling I'm so lonely without you*
*Can't sleep at night always thinking about you*
*But if I had the chance to start all over*
*I would be wishing today on a four-leaf clover*
*And leaving would be the last thing on my mind*
*If I could turn back the hands of time…*

(Okay, there were other more scholarly quotes that I could have used, but I happen to like Tyrone Davis).

Yes, don't we all wish at some point in our lives that we could turn back the hands of time? Most of us were young and foolish, but that is partly the definition of youth. Oscar Wilde said that youth is wasted on the young. How very true. I remember so vividly in my 20's working as a legal secretary and attending college; I thought I knew it all. I used to have discussions with my father, and he would tell me "There is enough that you don't know to make a whole new world." I always laughed at this remark, but as I matured and gained more experience, I realized what he was really saying. Maybe not enough to make a 'whole new world' but pretty darn close! We make bad calls and decisions, we sometimes don't listen to those who have life experience and we say to ourselves, "Sure, they made the mistake of doing this or doing that, but I know better." Then in hindsight, after we have traveled the same road, we find out that some situations could have been avoided had we only listened. We spent days going around a mountain when the same trip could have taken mere hours had we only taken the advice of someone who tried to guide us.

I can remember talking with my grandmother. She loved to read. There would always be piles of books on shelves and lining the walls of her room. She had books on just about every genre and subject. I loved sitting on the floor just watching her and listening to her recount stories from her youth and giving me sound advice. Sometimes I would get distracted and she would notice and say to me, "You're not paying me any more attention than a cat in Italy." As I did with my father, I would giggle every time she made this remark. I never thought to ask her what it meant – it sounded so funny and I just assumed it was an 'old folks' saying. Years later when I travelled to Italy, I noticed that almost everyone owned a dog. The cat population was very sparse. Upon returning home, I did some research and found that indeed there are cats in Italy, but in some areas such as the one I visited, they were far and in between. I realized at that point what my grandmother was saying. She had only been as far as Memphis and Chicago, but through reading so many books she had gained knowledge far beyond what I ever knew.

Now, this may be after the fact for a lot of you reading this, but others may be reading it at just the right time. Yes, everyone will make mistakes – to err is human. But when someone is imparting wisdom, be willing to listen with an open mind because they have already been where you are trying to go.

Inspiration: Take Life One Step At A Time

## Do's And Don'ts

DO toot your own horn. It is perfectly acceptable. Pat yourself on the back, applaud yourself loudly, and say "Bravo!"

DO learn to be comfortable in your own skin.

DO be uniquely you… and be good at it.

DO step outside of your comfort zone. Falling down is okay as long as you get back up and keep it moving.

DO take chances. That is the only way you will learn.

DO turn negatives into positives; turn losses into gains.

DO unplug from time to time. Take some deep breaths. Try meditation.

DO set up guardrails. That is, surround yourself with a good support system – people who can help you to advance. Someone once said that if you are the smartest person in the room, then you are in the wrong room.

DON'T let anyone tell you that you can't succeed. Remember, misery loves company.

DON'T get paralyzed. It took me a number of years to finish college. Some semesters I only took one class, but that was another one under my belt.

DON'T dwell on negative thoughts. Give them a day and a night, and let them go.

DON'T get discouraged. If a door closes in your face, go through the window. There's more than one way to skin a cat.

DON'T be a doormat. Remember, you teach people how to treat you.

DON'T become stagnant. Sometimes you may have to reinvent yourself. Change careers if you must.

Inspiration: Take Life One Step At A Time

## Learn To Strategize

I have always loved playing Scrabble, but I learned early on that there is more to it than just being able to spell. You can have all vowels or all consonants in your hand, but if you know the list of two-letter words you can still score some decent points. You also need to know how to place the letters on the board to not only score, but also to block your opponent. You need to be familiar enough with the rules to know that you can place a letter at the beginning *and* the ending of a word that is already on the board. Try to place your letters on Double Letter, Double Word, Triple Letter or Triple Word spaces to maximize your points. There are also two blank tiles in the game that can be used when needed and can count for any letter. My brother-in-law once asked me, "Are you a player or just a playette? There's a difference."

In this game called life, there is strategy involved. Our opponent (Satan) is playing for keeps. We pull letters, he pulls letters. We lay our letters on the board to score the highest possible points and he does the same. Sometimes we may have very little strength (all vowels or all consonants) but if we are familiar enough with the rules (the Word of God) we can find the best possible place to put those letters. Sometimes we may just have a two-letter word, but we know where to play those letters to score the highest number of points and stay in the game. We have to know how to use whatever letters we have in our hand to block our opponent. We step up our game and we learn to strategize. We use the two blank tiles (prayer and fasting) to place anywhere on the board to become whatever letters we need them to be. We lay them down when we really need them, and when our opponent least expects it. So step up your game; learn to strategize!

## Clean Out Your Closet

Let's say your mind is a closet. You need to organize your thoughts just as you would the clothes in your closet. Hang all the dresses together in one section, skirts in another, blouses or shirts in yet another area, and trousers would all hang together. Shoes don't go on hangers, they go on the floor or on a shoe rack in one section of the closet. Organize your mind. Remember, if your thoughts are jumbled and all over the place, so is your life. Take inventory of your 'closet' -- if something is no longer being worn or used, throw it out. Keep everything neat and clean. No ill-fitting outfits should be kept around. Is anybody listening? There is no need for things to take up space in your closet when they can be replaced with something more appropriate. Don't continue to try to wear an outfit if it does not 'fit' you anymore. It will only make you look bad. Oh can you hear me? Either have it altered or simply discard it. Rid your closet of anything that is just 'hanging around' and adding nothing to your wardrobe. That's right, rid yourself of people in your life who are just hanging around, taking up valuable space in your 'closet.' They are faded and out of shape and do nothing for you. Replace them with things that fit and make you look good. When you look in the mirror after getting dressed, you make any needed adjustments to your outfit. So go ahead - examine your life in a mirror and make any needed adjustments. Clean out your closet.

## *PART TWO*

## THOUGHTS TO CONSIDER

****************************

## Thoughts...

When a train goes through a tunnel and it's dark for a while, you don't get up and jump off. You sit still and trust the engineer. *Trust the process.*

Lord, above all, give me patience. Help me to remember that with you <u>all things</u> are possible. You are the chief engineer. I can only see what is directly in front of me. But you have an aerial view and know what is miles ahead. You have already prepared me for it.

*"And we know that all things work together for good to them that love God, to them who are the called according to his purpose." Romans 8:28 (KJV)*

## **More Thoughts…**

Talk about a *REAL* Valentine -- God is such a gentleman. He always opens doors for me. When I'm not quite there, he waits and holds the door for me. He politely makes suggestions on the right way to go, but if I go astray he is right there waiting when I realize my mistake, and he doesn't say "I told you so." No matter what time of night, he's always willing to chat. Once I got extremely ticked off at him to the point where I wouldn't speak for a while. Oh, it was ugly! But when I finally cooled off, he said "You know that was for your good, right?" And I had to agree. He is loyal to a fault, and really understands me better than anyone. Yes... such a gentleman. I'm in love.

*"Love is patient, love is kind. It does not envy, it does not boast, it is not proud. It does not dishonor others, it is not self-seeking. It is not easily angered, it keeps no record of wrongs." 1 Corinthians 13: 4-5 (NIV)*

## **Musings...**

Learning never stops. Be open to meeting new people and respecting their opinions. Everyone has a point of view. Everyone has a story to tell. Enrich your life by broadening your surroundings and your circle of friends.

*******************

When God shuts a door, stop banging on it.

*******************

Tell the negative committee that meets inside your head to sit down and shut up.

*******************

Sometimes God will deliver us out of the fire -- then other times he will make us fire-proof.

*******************

## **Further Thoughts**…

Pay close attention to those who *don't* clap when you win. Surround yourself with people who are excited for you.

*******************

Don't allow anyone to live in your head rent-free.

*******************

Destroy negative thoughts when they first appear, for that is when they are the weakest.

*******************

Never give up on your dreams. And by all means, never underestimate yourself. When The Wizard of Oz came out in 1939, it was considered a box office failure. Need I say more?

Inspiration: Take Life One Step At A Time

## **Consider this…**

Favor gives you VIP status. Favor keeps you focused (Psalms 5:12)

The favor of God has PURPOSE. (Psalms 106)

*******************

Pay close attention to what people *don't* say - discernment is a beautiful thing.

*******************

God gives us 2nd, 3rd, 4th, 5th and more chances. It took Enoch 300 years! KEEP WALKING!!!

*******************

In all thy ways, acknowledge Him, and he shall direct thy paths. **WATCH THE DIRECTOR.**

*******************

Debrief – Meditate – Exhale – Relax – Repeat.

## **Memories**...

Old songs come to mind that my mother used to sing – "I know the Bible is right and somebody's wrong." And… "So many falling by the wayside, Lord help me stand; I don't want to be lost when Jesus comes!"

*"Jesus Christ the same yesterday, and today and forever." Hebrews 13:8 (KJV)*

## **Remember**...

Love your family unconditionally. Never forget those that raised you and taught you life's core values. Continue to make them proud and don't let their legacy die.

## **Know this**…

I am nothing without God. If he took one step away from me, I would fall flat on my face. This realization keeps me grounded and humble. One of my favorite old songs: 'Without Him I would be nothing. Without Him I would fail. Without Him I

## Inspiration: Take Life One Step At A Time

would be drifting. Like a ship without a sail.'

Sylvia Carlton

Seasons come and seasons go. A new year begins and before we know it spring is here, followed by summer, then fall and winter, and we are left asking where did the time go? I have found that by having a focus for every month, it brings more clarity and helps to remind me to be thankful for each new day. Even though time moves swiftly, we still need to stop and smell the flowers as much as we can. With that being said, I am sharing my observations and thoughts for each month of the year.

## **PART THREE**

## MONTH BY MONTH ENCOURAGEMENT

*****************************

## JANUARY

Before we know it, another year is being ushered in. Time doesn't stop marching, although we sometimes wish we could slow it down just a bit. What's done is done. Yesterday - even one minute ago - is in the past and there is no rewind button. We make plans for the future, as we should, but we have no choice but to live in the moment. *What do I know for sure?* I know that sometimes the best laid plans do not pan out, and we have to be able to regroup, gather our thoughts and move on. So celebrate each day, bring out the umbrella when it rains in your life, and when the rain stops, enjoy the beautiful rainbow. And remember, January 1$^{st}$ is the first page of a 365-page book. Write a good one.

## FEBRUARY

We like to celebrate Valentine's Day in February with love being the central theme. Love your family because they are the ones who will rescue you when that Mack truck hits you. Cherish your friends because they will listen without judging you. *What I know for sure is this–* if you are genuinely happy for the success of others, yours will soon follow. So, during February, and every month, remember to celebrate each day for the wonderful gift that it is.

## MARCH

I've always been a good judge of character. People rarely surprise me. That being said, I would like to share that I recently had the pleasure of having breakfast with a terrific group of ladies of varying ages, interests and backgrounds. They are all members of my church and even though I see each of them every Sunday, I actually know very little about them. We shared a little of our backgrounds, likes and dislikes, funny stories and serious issues. How refreshing the conversation was. And how appropriate that we met just as the month of March came in. The weather is breaking, days are a bit sunnier, and doesn't that just generally improve your disposition? That's certainly how I felt when I left our meeting. So yes, people rarely surprise me. But I was pleasantly surprised to learn more about my sisters and share more about myself as well. *Here's what is for sure* – you can't judge a book by its cover and there is always more to learn about people.

## APRIL

April showers bring May flowers. Is that how the saying goes? I guess it depends upon what part of the world you live in. Well, let's just say that it does. But let's say that April could be any month or any period of time. Whenever there has been a time of showers in your life, the flowers have bloomed afterwards. When the flowers appear in all their beauty, we don't forget the rainy days but we do realize that the showers had to occur in order to reap such a beautiful outcome. Yes, you know where I'm going with this. It's not new. You've heard it before. After a rainy season, we have to admit that all that water was very much needed whether we enjoyed it or not. Moving into the spring of the year the trees are budding, the ground is getting warmer and the birds are returning. It is a process of nature and it's always orchestrated quite well. *What do I know for sure?* I know that simply waking up is cause for celebration. I know for sure that whenever showers come in your life, they will always be followed by flowers.


## **MAY**

"Just Keep Living." This was always my father's reply when I was impatient with him for being too slow, or antsy about a situation, or didn't understand why he made certain decisions. There were many instances when he would say those words, but one in particular that I

## Inspiration: Take Life One Step At A Time

will never forget was when I was in grammar school. He would give us our weekly allowance on Sunday nights. This included lunch money, spending money and milk money. Some of you I'm sure remember those days when cartons of milk were delivered to the school and you could pay 3 cents a day for white milk or 4 cents a day for chocolate milk. He would sit at the kitchen table and count out our allowance and it seemed like it took forever. I would always complain, "Daddy, why do you count so slow?" To which he would reply, "Just keep living." Fast forward 45-plus years. I did keep living, and some days it brings tears to my eyes when I remember all those times when my father said those words. But if my daddy could see me now, I believe I would make him proud. Indeed, I have kept living and yes now I understand in so many situations exactly what he meant. I had to laugh out loud just the other day when I found myself counting out some money to one of my nieces, and I could tell by the look on her face that she wanted to say "Syl, can't you count any faster?" It would have made my day if she had actually asked me that, and I could have replied, "Just keep living." *So here's what is for sure*: if we are blessed to live long enough, we appreciate what our parents taught us. We fall and we get back up and we keep living and before we know it, we are at that spot. Some things are not understood until we get on the other side of the street, so to speak. Some things can only come to be understood with the passage of time. Life is grand, not perfect, but wonderful nonetheless. So take the good with the bad and just keep living!

## JUNE

If I were to do a little spring cleaning, I would start with first reflecting on January through May. What am I holding on to that I really could discard? Maybe a little, hopefully not a lot. But you know how it is when you prepare to move and start pulling things out. You stand back and say, "Good Lord! When did I accumulate all of this?" That's because we have gone for long periods of time without sorting through some things and letting go of what we don't need. So as I begin sorting through the first half of this year, I will go room by room and bring out what I really don't need. Get rid of what is just taking up space. Let go of what I haven't used in a long time. Get rid of the old and make room for the new. This is not always easy because we tend to hold on to things thinking we will use them. *What do I know for sure?* I know that there is only so much that I can hold on to for so long and then it's purging time. Out with the old and in with the new. That includes situations and people. I know that I must keep it moving with expectancy and not become stagnant. So, join me and let's clean it up and clear it out!

## JULY

The recent Supreme Court Ruling regarding same-sex marriage has everyone talking. We all have our own feelings and opinions on the subject. It is being debated and discussed at work, at school, at church, on the train, in stores, at hair salons -- practically everywhere. Of course, it's over and done and cannot be reversed, but it has certainly woke everyone up. As a writer, I know that remaining neutral is sometimes in my best interest. On the other hand, just as I have characters in my head demanding to be heard, I have to voice my opinion on this all-important issue. I personally do not condone same-sex marriage, but people are people and everyone deserves to be happy however they choose. I am neither judge nor jury, but in the 5/4 vote, my vote would have been part of the 4. This ruling greatly affects the next generation's thinking and morals. It is up to us to instill in them what we believe is right and be prepared to explain the reasons why. *I know for sure that life as we know it has changed because of this ruling. The world is ever changing and will continue to do so, but God is constant and his word remains the same no matter how we change.*

## AUGUST

I recently had a very interesting conversation with my brother. We were discussing delayed blessings. There really is no such thing; it's just that God's timing is not our timing. Case in point: If you have ever been prescribed Vitamin D, you know that you take a tablet only once a week. Seems like a long period between doses, but because the pills are so potent, that is all it takes. You are cautioned to wait a full seven days between each pill, because if you take them any closer together your body cannot process it. The medicine is working over a full week, slowly but surely, although you may not feel it. At the end of the prescribed period, be it a month or more, you will see the results. Sometimes God gives us Vitamin D blessings. We send up prayers daily, attend church weekly, read and meditate daily but may still feel that our prayers are not being heard. Just wait. The Vitamin D is working. He can't give it to us all at once because we wouldn't be able to process it. But over a period of time, when enough Vitamin D has been taken (prayers, meditations, reading the Word) and built up in our system, we will see the results. *What does this tell me for sure?* I know and understand that God sees the whole picture; the beginning and the ending. We need only to believe and trust the process. Just take the Vitamin D and don't skip any doses and we will get the desired results.

## SEPTEMBER

During 2015, I have posted on Facebook on the first day of every month with my thoughts, reflections and views. Little did I know that in September I would be reflecting on the life of a very dear family member. My aunt made her transition in August of 2015. You know how all the cousins have that favorite aunt? Well, she was the one. She was classy, elegant, witty, charming, smart and humorous, and she loved life. If I could be even half the woman she was, it would be phenomenal. *I know for sure* that her living was not in vain. I know that the values she instilled in us will never die. I know that her teaching and instruction made me a better woman. *What we all know for sure* is that talk is cheap. It's what you *do* that matters. My aunt taught by example. She showed us how a real wife and mother took care of business. She demonstrated how an aunt could be a best friend to a niece. She portrayed how to gain respect and keep it. She went above and beyond the call of duty and left her footprints on this planet. There can never be another one like her.

## OCTOBER

Well, I guess *one thing I know for sure* is that time is speeding by. It's not waiting for any of us. I know for sure that what I once thought was comical is not so funny after all. One aunt told me in my early twenties that one day little reminder notes would be my best friend. I thought this was oh so funny, but how right she was. An older co-worker admonished me to take advantage of all the savings incentives offered by the company. She had not done so and when she "looked around" it was 30 years later. Yes, I know for sure that the older we get, the faster the years fly by. I also surely know that the longer we live, the more precious life is and this includes the value of family and friends. So welcome October. Enjoy the changing colors. Embrace the cooler days and grab that comforter for those chilly nights. Appreciate the season even if it's not your favorite. Because we know for sure that it will come and go just like that. *That's for sure.*

## NOVEMBER

This is the month that we traditionally celebrate Thanksgiving. Yes, there is so much to be thankful for. Life, health, family, a sound mind, friends, shelter, and the list goes on. Every single morning as soon as my eyes open, I thank God for waking me up. *I know for sure*, and especially of late, that just waking up should not be taken for granted. And after waking up, taking a shower, dressing, and driving my car are all small miracles that I am truly thankful for. I know that as I enjoy my Thanksgiving dinner later this month, there are those who will not be doing the same. Yes, I am obligated to share with others who are less fortunate than myself. *What do I know?* I know that I must continue to be thankful and grateful for whatever I have and in doing so, I will be blessed to be a blessing to others.

## DECEMBER

Deck The Halls, Silent Night, We Three Kings… yes, it's Christmas. The time of year when our minds turn to shopping and gift giving and making merry and eating way too much. Department stores and the Hallmark Channel start advertising Christmas at the end of October. I just recently returned downtown to work, and the decorations on Michigan Avenue are absolutely beautiful. The window displays and ornaments on the trees are bright and festive. But even more beautiful than that is God's decoration – the falling snowflakes and the miracle that no two are alike, the crisp clean air, the trees with snow resting on the branches.

*This I know for sure:* every day that I wake up is a cause for celebration. I am blessed with the gift of life each and every morning. I am decorated with the ornaments of grace and mercy. The Word of God that I read upon waking is a perpetual Christmas card that brings greetings of joy and happiness.

What else do I know for sure? I know that Christmas commemorates the birth of Christ and that we celebrate that birthday every year. We send cards and give gifts to those we love to show how much we care. Deck the Halls, Silent Night, We Three Kings – while we sing these beautiful melodies, let us remember the true meaning and reason for the season. Let us all know for sure that without Christ there is no Christmas.

## PART FOUR

## #LOVINGJOE
## #IWILLSURVIVE

\*\*\*\*\*\*\*\*\*\*\*\*\*\*\*\*\*\*\*\*\*\*\*\*\*\*\*\*

I was undecided about whether to include this section, but after giving it some thought I decided that this is the perfect place for it to be shared. This book is about encouraging and inspiring and I hope that in sharing my experience it may help someone who may have suffered a tremendous loss.

Joe-Joe was my great-nephew, and the closest thing to a son that I had. (I have no biological children.) We shared so many wonderful times together; he actually lived with me for a short time during his life. He passed away in January, 2016 at the age of 20.

Not until tragedy strikes do you discover how strong you are. It is easy to console others during their time of trouble, but when it hits home, then it becomes the true litmus test.

Tuesday, January 5, 2016 started out like any other winter day in Chicago. It was crisp and cold and the perfect day to stay home. However, I did not have that luxury, so I bundled up and headed out for work. I had no idea as I drove to the train that by nightfall this would turn out to be the most tragic day of my life. What I never told anyone until now was that I had the worst feeling of foreboding all day long. I can remember praying and asking God to cover me and my family with his divine protection. At one point during the day, I became so anxious that I had to get up from my desk and walk outside. As the day wore on, the feeling of doom and gloom continued to intensify. No matter how hard I tried, I could not shake it. I began to pray even more and ask God to give me strength to endure whatever was about to happen.

I started to go by my sister's house after work, but then decided instead that I should go home and then to church. As I would later find out, everything happens in divine order, and it was definitely not meant for me to be at her house when the events of that evening unfolded. After eating dinner, I headed for church. I still felt anxious and tense, so at this point I began to blame it on the weather. After all, it was a cold and gray winter day. That had to be it -- just the winter blahs. While driving home from church, my phone rang and I looked over and saw that the call was from my sister Doris. Immediately my stomach dropped and somehow I knew that this was a call that I did not want to receive. I now knew that this was the reason for how I had been feeling all day.

I pulled over and picked up the phone. My sister was in hysterics, telling me that the garage was on fire and Joe-Joe was trapped inside. It was then that I knew why I should not have been at the house. I did not need to see him brought out of the garage. God knows how much we can bear. At the hospital, we were told that he would probably not survive through the night. He actually did live until that Friday, January 8th, when he transitioned peacefully that evening.

I mentioned in my earlier remarks about how Everlene Hampton, a priceless friend, was such a Godsend during the time when I lost Joe-Joe. About a month after the tragedy, she came to me and said "I am going to purchase a journal for you and I want you to write something every day for an entire year. Even on the days that you don't feel like writing, just write down your thoughts. Write how you are feeling, write about the weather, write down memories of Joe-Joe. Whatever you do, don't go one day without writing something." I can remember looking at her with tears streaming down my face thinking she must be crazy. How in the world could I write anything? Most days I had to remind myself to breathe. I was living not one day at a time, but literally one minute at a time. How did she expect me to put a pen to paper? But what she knew was that it was important for me to keep writing, even through the pain. It was important for me to keep writing so that my gift would not die. So I did as she said and I wrote something in the journal every single day for an entire year. At first it was extremely painful. There were days when all I could do was write one sentence and put the journal away. But I continued to write, and slowly I began to realize how it was helping me. It was a huge part of my healing process.

Oftentimes we may not see things clearly at first, especially when we are in the midst of a trial. Even though my heart was breaking as I wrote, I did as Everlene had instructed. Near the end of the year, I went back and read what I had written at the beginning. I saw how broken I was and how I became just a bit stronger each day. I could see the healing process as it unfolded. Early on, I was only able to write down a single thought. But months in, I began to construct full paragraphs and express my feelings more and more. During that year, however, I was hurting so intensely that I was still unable to complete any chapters for my book, but the important thing was that I was writing something every day, and I realized that was the point of it all.

I've had several of what I call "Joe-Joe" days. I recorded my thoughts on those days and would like to share some of them here:

***Joe-Joe...*** On January 5th, you decided that you wanted to leave. We tried to hold on to you, but on January 8th we had to let you go. It would have been unbearable to keep watching the machine breathe for you, so on that day you took your last breath on your own. I have had such a range of emotions, and there were a few times when I thought I just wouldn't wake up the next morning. But by the grace of God, one day at a time, I am still here. I miss you so much. I miss everything about you. I never imagined I could feel this much pain. I know that you did not mean to hurt us so badly, so I forgive you. If you could undo it, I know that you would. I have gone through the five stages of grief back and forth several times. Nothing could have prepared me for this. I just never saw it coming. Some days are unbearable, others are just okay. Keep watching over me my angel and come visit me sometime.***

***Can't sleep...*** I have been having a lot of those nights. I've always been able to fall asleep as soon as my head hit the pillow and not wake up even once during

## Inspiration: Take Life One Step At A Time

the night. Ahhhh... life. It catches us off guard and throws curve balls at us. We get knocked down (and in my case, it feels like a cement roller has flattened me out) but somehow we get back up and keep going. From somewhere we find strength to make it through another day. So many days since Joe-Joe left I have no idea how I got to work and back home, and I have no memory of what I did while I was at work. I don't know how long this grieving process will take. I'm writing this more for myself than anyone else. It just has to come out. I'm reading all the suicide survivor books and materials I can get my hands on, but none of them have been able to tell me why Joe-Joe left me. I've asked him to come visit me, but I think that he feels I'm not ready for that yet. He may be right. The Bible tells me that all things work together for good...it doesn't say that we will understand all things. So I'm just holding on to that and telling myself that everything is in divine order. *Though billows roll, He keeps my soul. My heavenly father watches over me.*\*\*\*

*****Memories...** So many memories. Every morning I think about you. I have prayed that you not be the first thought on my mind when I wake up, but so far you still are. Maybe one day you won't be. I've been to a counseling session and it helped tremendously, but I just wish I didn't have to go in the first place. I post about you, but I'm trying to slow down with that. I guess there are really no rules to follow; no time limit on grief. I would never have believed this level of pain existed. I want to get back to my writing, but that part of my brain has not been able to work again yet. I pray as best I can, all throughout the day, so I can try to function as normally as possible. I just spoke with a client, and she ended the conversation by saying, "It's a gloomy day, but I wish you sunshine." Mind you, this woman didn't know me from Adam, but she spoke life to me. I was in a dark place today -- having a really tough day. I hung up the phone and took a walk around the block even though it looked like rain, and as I did, the sun came out. God is awesome! I love you and miss you. I hope you are at peace.*****

Inspiration: Take Life One Step At A Time

**\*\*\*Nothing like losing someone to put things into perspective...** It matters not what the weather is, I'm just thankful for waking up. I'm at the end of a contract on my job, but I trust God. My clothes are not designer, but they are clean. My family is around me for support, as are my friends. Aside from a few aches, my health is good. Yes, I'm hurting for I am human. I now understand why people go on like this. Not for 'likes' or comments, but for themselves. It has to come out. But this too shall pass.\*\*\*

**\*\*\*It's Halloween and I'm really missing Joe-Joe today, big time...** I used to take him trick or treating every year. He really looked forward to it. Oh my how he loved candy! I would rush home from work to take him and his best friend. I honestly think I enjoyed it more than they did. But I think I hear him telling me, "Don't cry Aunty-Mommy. Just be happy when you think about me." So today I'm smiling. I promise you Joe-Joe. No tears.\*\*\*

**\*\*\*Angel On My Shoulder...** So now I have my very own personal angel who is with me always. No, this is not the way I want him; of course, I want him here in the flesh. But this is the way it is, and I am grateful that he is still near me even if in a different form. There he is each morning, telling me to get up and get going and please don't cry. There he is again in the evening when the sun starts to set and I start to feel sad telling me it's okay and he is okay. Angel on my shoulder. My Joe-Joe, my one and only, forever in my heart. I love you so much.***

## **Final Thoughts**

If you're happy and you know it clap your hands. If you're happy and you know it, then you really ought to show it. If you're happy and you know it clap your hands. No, I have not reverted to being five years old. Although it is mostly true that everything we need to know we learned in kindergarten. We were taught how to play well with others, how to share, how to respect others and their opinions and property, and even how to take a nap to recharge your body. So goes life. But along the way you learn how to take the good with the bad, how to adjust to the ups and downs, how to push through adversity, and how to see the glass half full instead of half empty. So you keep living life one day at a time. You have some great moments and some not-so-great moments. You celebrate yourself and others. You clap your hands. You keep it moving. You dance like nobody's watching -- and if you stumble... make it part of the dance!

*******************

Sylvia Carlton

Labels on many products often read 'Best if used by...' Well, I've found that prayer is best if used by early morning. That's not to say that it will expire, but there is just something about talking to God early in the morning. Early in the morning before the cares of the day start to surface. Bright and early while it is still quiet. Earlier than the trains, and the traffic, and the demands on our day. While the dew is still on the roses. Yes, prayer -- best if used upon rising, and it also can be re-applied as needed throughout the day.

*******************

In my career as a legal assistant, the most important part of my job was not typing, or preparing closing books, or putting together witness files, or even appearing in court. No, the most important aspect of the job was FILING. That's right, if a document was misfiled, it could literally make or break a case. It was a task that no one enjoyed, but it was a necessary evil. So it is in life. We do not always want to take the time to file things in their proper place. We all need to file away some family time where we actually lay our phones down and talk to each other. Try opening a new file to put in people that you don't normally associate with at work, at church or at school. You may be pleasantly surprised by how much you have in common. We all really do need to expand the "P" file and increase our prayer life. With everything that's going on around us, this file itself should take up at least two drawers in the filing cabinet. I trust that this blesses you. If not, then just file it away and come back to it later.

*******************

Finally, make sure you always travel on a one-way street so that it is impossible for you to go back. Don't pull into any parking spots. Even if the road is uphill or rocky, just keep going. Even if your tires have very little tread, just keep pushing. Don't apply the brakes. Even though the gage is almost on "E" and you may be running on fumes, trust me on this – there will be a service station right there when you need it. Pull in, fill up your tank, put some air in the tires, and keep going.

\*\*\*\*\*\*\*\*\*\*\*\*\*\*\*\*\*\*\*\*\*\*\*\*\*\*\*\*

I sincerely hope you enjoyed this compilation. Please feel free to share your comments and thoughts with me at **sylvia.carlton@ymail.com**. I would love to hear from you.

Inspiration: Take Life One Step At A Time

**Now, as promised, here is an excerpt from my upcoming novel "Colors."**

Angela sat in her Physics class listening to the instructor drone on about light and energy and electricity. It was such a beautiful day and she was finding it hard to concentrate. She could care less at this point about how matter and energy related. The subject of matter just didn't matter and she had no energy. The clock seemed to be moving in slow motion. It was the first week of May and the semester would be over in just a few short days. She was looking forward to beginning her senior year at San Antonio South Academy. Where had the time gone? It seemed only yesterday that she and her twin brother Aaron had entered high school.

The vibration of Angela's cell phone snapped her out of her reverie. She glanced down and saw that it was a text from her father, James Burke, asking her to call home. That was strange. What was it that could not wait until she got home? Maybe he wanted her to stop and pick up something on her way in. She tried to dismiss it, but yet she had an uneasy feeling, much like the sixth sense that one has when something just isn't right.

Angie met her twin brother Aaron in the hallway after class. "Aaron" she frowned, "I got a text from Dad saying to call home. What do you think that's about?" "Beats me," Aaron chuckled as he shoved his back pack in his locker. Aaron never brought books home and seldom studied, but somehow managed to get straight A's. He often teased Angie that he was the twin with the brains and she was the one with the beauty. Just then, her cell phone rang; it was her Dad calling. Angie's palms began to sweat as she answered. "Hi dad, what's going on?" She could hear the apprehension in her father's voice as he spoke slowly, "Angie, sweetie, there's been an accident. Mom was flying in from Houston this afternoon and the plane went down. They haven't released any names yet. You and Aaron need to meet me at the hospital."

\* \* \*

Have you ever associated people with colors? If James Burke was a color, he would be purple – strong, stoic, royal. But on this day, he was more gray than anything else. Still, dull, and moving robotically. Aaron would be the color green. The color of life. He was always energized, well-liked by his peers, and an all-around good guy and athlete who made school seem effortless. But today, he resembled a small frightened child as they walked toward the hospital emergency room entrance. 'In the pink' is a phrase that means feeling good and doing well. That was Angie to a tee. But on this day, Angie's world had turned black in a matter of minutes…

**"COLORS" WILL BE COMING YOUR WAY SOON!**

www.ingramcontent.com/pod-product-compliance
Lightning Source LLC
Chambersburg PA
CBHW032213040426
42449CB00005B/581